Grade **2.2**

Scott Foresman

Decodable
Practice Readers
16A - 30C
Volume 2

Scott Foresman
is an imprint of

Glenview, Illinois • Boston, Massachusetts • Chandler, Arizona
• Upper Saddle River, New Jersey

ISBN-13: 978-0-328-49218-3
ISBN-10:   0-328-49218-3
12 13 14 15 V011 17 16 15 14 13
CC1

Contents

UNIT 5

UNIT 6

The Lunch Table

Written by Laura Susin

Final Syllable -*le*

simple	table	able	purple
sparkle	handle	puddle	bundle
tickle	candle	giggle	

High-Frequency Words

set	table	today
able	water	

1

It's time to eat.
It is simple to set this table.
Pam is able to do it
by herself.

2

First, Pam sets purple dishes
on her table.
Pam likes purple.
Today is a nice day for purple.

Pam sets glasses on the table.
They sparkle in the sunlight.
Pam gets napkins too.
Her napkins match the purple plates.
It is fun setting the table!

4

Pam holds the jug of
water by the handle.
She will not spill.
There will be no puddle!

This table needs
a bundle of roses.
Won't this table smell nice?
Roses tickle Pam's nose!

Last, this table needs a candle on it.
Mom will light that candle.
After that, Mom can finish
making lunch.
Pam can't wait to eat!

The table is set.
Mom sets lunch on the table.
Pam and Mom fixed lunch as a team!
It makes Pam giggle to think
of how she was able to help.

Anna's Fable

Final Syllable –le

Tuttle	Fables	simple	riddles
puzzles	settled	table	little
turtle	fiddle	maple	juggle
pebbles	single	nibble	bubble
trickle	able	struggle	

High-Frequency Words

table	today	turn	want
tree	find	water	able
show			

Mister Tuttle is teaching fables in class. A fable is a tale that teaches a lesson. Some lessons might be simple. Some lessons may be more like riddles or puzzles. Last night, Anna settled in at her kitchen table.

Her homework was to make up a fable.

Today in class, it was Anna's turn to tell her fable. In her fable, a little turtle plays his fiddle rather than tackling winter chores. Turtle didn't want to work, just play that fiddle under his maple tree. Sometimes Turtle stopped fiddling just to juggle little pebbles. But when winter came, Turtle did not find a single thing to nibble, nor a bubble or trickle of water to drink.

In her fable, Anna is able to show that it is better to work hard in summer, than struggle in winter.

The Maple Tree

Written by Kara Linden

Final Syllable *-le*

maple	simple	stumble
table	bottle	bubbles
able	puddle	giggle

High-Frequency Words

seen	tree	find
show	turn	want

11

Have you seen that old maple tree?
It's simple to find the maple tree.
Stan can show the way!
He can run fast.
Can you?

12

Run by this big rock.
Do not stumble!
Turn right when you
pass this rock.

Kids are playing hopscotch.
It's not a hard game to play.
Run by that game.
Sit at that table.

14

It's time to rest!
We'll find the maple tree,
but first we'll drink the water
in this bottle.

Kids are blowing bubbles!
We will blow bubbles too.
Stan is able to blow big bubbles.

Off we go!
Jump over that big puddle
but don't step in.
Keep running.
The hardest part is over.

This is it!
This is the big maple tree for you to see.
We can sit under this tree.
We can giggle under this tree.
Why did you want to find this tree?

A Good Book

Written by Quinn Hart

Vowel Patterns *oo, u*

book(s)	look	good	looking
stood	looked	cook	cookbook
took	put	full	

High-Frequency Words

| get | book | for | these |
| ask | maybe | down | seat |

Mike has a card
that he uses to get books.
What kind of book
will he look for?

20

Mike runs up these steps.
He sees books, books,
and more books!
Can Mike find a good book?

21

Mike will ask the man at this desk.
"I'm looking for a book," Mike said.
"A book? We have lots of books!
What kind do you want?" he asked.

"I am looking for a good book,"
Mike said as he stood
and looked at books.
"Maybe I'll read this book.
It will teach me how to cook!"

Mike will check out this cookbook!
The man took Mike's card
and he took Mike's book.
Then he gave the book and card
back to Mike.

24

Mike put his bag down
and took a seat.
The book was full of good
things to eat.

Mike will take his book home.
He will cook with his mom!
Mike is on his way
to being a good cook!

Cookbooks

Vowel Patterns *oo, u*

butcher	Bush	cook
pushed	books	cooking
cookbooks	look	pudding
footlong	wood	pulled
took	put	nook
rookie	fulfilled	

High-Frequency Words

asked	for	maybe	book
box	down	these	lake
fish	get	seat	

Sam the butcher finished his day's work at Mister Bush's store. Sam liked his job, but he asked Mister Bush for a job as a cook.

"Maybe," said Mister Bush. He pushed Sam to read books on

27

cooking. Sam took home a box of cookbooks.

On his way home that night, Sam sat down in his bus and looked at his books. These books told about cooking things from pudding to footlong hot dogs. His last book told him how to cook fresh lake fish on a wood fire.

The bus pulled into Sam's stop. He had to get up from his seat. Sam took his books home. He put them in his kitchen nook, but took one to read each day. In just weeks, Mister Bush gave Sam a job as a rookie cook!

Sam fulfilled his wish!

Kevin Hooks a Fish

Written by Natalie Lohrman

Vowel Patterns *oo, u*

brook	full	shook	stood
look	hooks	put	hook
pulled	hooked		

High-Frequency Words

fish	let's	full
lake	box	

29

Max and Kevin felt bored.
"Let's fish at the brook," said Kevin.
"No, let's fish at the lake,"
said Max.
"It is full of fish."

"Are the fishing poles
in this box?" asked Max.
Kevin shook the big box.
His poles fell out.
"Let's go," he said.

"Look!" yelled Kevin.
"The lake is close!
Let's race to that tree."
Kevin and Max ran to the tree
that stood by the lake.

32

Kevin and Max checked
their fishing hooks.
"Let's put our lines in," said Max.
They dropped the fishing lines in.

Kevin and Max stood for
a long time waiting for fish.
"When will those fish bite?"
asked Max.

Then there was a splash and a tug.
"I have a fish on my hook!"
yelled Kevin.
Kevin pulled hard on his line.

Kevin hooked a big lake fish!
When will Max hook a big
lake fish?

Joy's Flowers

Written by Donyette Sanchez

Diphthongs *ou, ow, oi, oy*

Joy	found	flower(s)
frown	soil	brown
now	how	pound
down	moist	shower
sprout	without	noise
out	ground	proud

High-Frequency Words

seeds	soil	plant
land	brown	

Joy found a bag of flower seeds.
What can she do with them?
Joy had a frown on her face.
Then she smiled.
She will make a garden in the soil!

What will she do first?
Joy will plant her seeds.
A good spot of land
is what Joy needs.

This soil is nice and brown.
Joy digs tiny holes
for the seeds.
She will dig holes
for every single one of them!

40

Now the seeds can be planted.
One seed in each hole
is how it's done.
Put soil on top,
but do not pound it down!

It's time to make the soil moist.
It is a shower for the flowers!
It will help them sprout.
Now they just need sunlight.

When will the flowers sprout?
Without a noise,
the flowers will poke out
of the ground and go up to the sky.

43

Joy is so proud!
Her flowers did get big.
She will pick one flower
and take it home.

44

Troy's Flowers

Diphthongs *ou, ow, oi, oy*

Troy	boy	house	amount
brown	ground	pointed	found
counted	out	loud	choice
soil	outside	flowers	downtown
plowed	showered	moist	toil
sprout	proud	enjoy	

High-Frequency Words

land	brown	wild
seeds	plant	soil
grow		

Troy was an older boy. Behind his house there was a large amount of land. It was good brown dirt filled with wild weeds. Troy pulled weeds out of that ground. He used a pointed weed puller he found.

Troy counted out loud as he pulled weeds.

Troy had a plan. A garden would be a good choice for the brown soil outside his house. Now that the weeds had been pulled out, flowers would be perfect!

Troy rode his bike downtown. He got seeds to plant in his brown soil. When he got back, he plowed the dirt a bit. Then Troy planted seeds. He showered his garden with water. Moist ground helped seeds grow.

Troy's toil paid off. Flowers began to sprout! Troy was proud! He would enjoy his flowers.

Cowboy Roy

Written by Julia Parrish

Diphthongs *ou, ow, oi, oy*

Roy	choice	cowboy(s)
around	ground	foil
cows	town	toys
spoiled	boy	joy
voice	join	noise

High-Frequency Words

grow	speak	ride
rope	wild	

"This is the day to tell
what you want to be
when you grow up!
Roy, will you speak first?"
the teacher asked.

48

What will Roy be?
Roy will tell the class his choice.
He will be a cowboy!

Roy will ride his horse around.
He will twirl his rope over
the ground.
He will herd those cows
and keep an eye on them.

Roy will protect the cows
from wild animals.
Maybe Roy will foil a plot
if some cows leave town.
He can save the herd!

Roy will give up his toys
to look after cows!
Roy is not a spoiled boy.
He thinks that being a cowboy
will bring him joy.

In his camp at night,
Roy will use his fine voice
to sing cowboy tunes
under the bright stars.

Yes! He will tell the class
how he will join other cowboys!
But Roy does not make a noise.
Roy is a very shy cowboy.

54

Boyhood Dreams

Janis Jay

Decodable
Practice
Reader
19A

Syllable Patterns

boyhood	cowboy	Seaweed
daydreams	oatmeal	roundups
cookouts	Loudmouth	southeast

High-Frequency Words

young
travel
direction
clear

Gramps told Gina about his boyhood dreams.
"When I was young, I dreamt about being a cowboy," he told her.

"I always saw myself riding an old horse named Seaweed," Gramps explained.

"Seaweed?" asked Gina.

"Yep," replied Gramps smiling.

"In my daydreams, I fed Seaweed oats.
I ate oatmeal.
Then we rode out on cattle roundups," added Gramps.

"We rode hard in daytime.
At night, we would enjoy cowboy
cookouts," said Gramps.

"Did you ever try to be a real
cowboy?" Gina asked.
"No, but once I rode an old horse,"
said Gramps with a bigger smile.

"This horse was named Loudmouth.
I tried to travel in a southeast
direction, but he didn't agree.
So we rode northwest," said
Gramps. Both he and Gina laughed.

"It was clear I would not be a good
cowboy!" Gramps said to Gina
Gina hugged Gramps.
"But you are a great granddad,"
she said.

Jack's Daydreams

Syllable Patterns

railroads	daydream
cowboy	football
bookkeeper	railway
steamboat	sailboat

High-Frequency Words

travel   wide

At night, Mom and Jack planned to watch an old show about railroads. But as the show started, power in the house and on the whole block went out. It was a blackout!

Mom grabbed her flashlight. Jack sat outside on his porch. In the dark, Jack started to daydream about growing up. At first, he saw himself as a cowboy or a football player. He might make a good bookkeeper like his dad.

Jack remembered the show about railroads. He might work for a railway. Then he asked himself if there were still steamboats. He would like to travel by steamboat in a wide river. Or he might travel on a sailboat.

Jack's mind ran from idea to idea. That was the fun of daydreaming!

When that blackout ended, Jack stayed on the porch. Daydreaming was more fun than TV!

Joy's Raincoat

Daniel Suh

Mom packed Joy's lunch bag.
It had a sandwich, apple and
oatmeal bar.
"Thanks, Mom," yelled Joy as she ran
out to the school bus.

As Joy ran, Mom saw that Joy had a
raincoat on her arm.
Mom looked out the townhouse
window.
The day was sunny and clear!

When Joy stepped on the bus, kids saw that she held a raincoat. Several kids were afraid that might mean bad weather later.

The bus rode through wide
downtown streets to Joy's school.
In class, Joy took her raincoat to her
desk.
Miss Best spotted it and smiled.

Joy's class read about farms and soybeans.
It saw a DVD about seaweed.
Then Miss Best played music and kids painted rainbows.

At recess, kids waited in line to get a drink.
When kids hit the button, water sprayed them.
"They still didn't fix that!" said Miss Best.

That's when Joy put on her raincoat.
"I'm ready for a drink today," she
said.
After her drink, Joy lent her raincoat
to her classmates.

Is It True?

Written by Meera Laurent

Vowel Digraphs *oo, ue, ew, ui*

Sue	true	moo	flew
moon	clue	too	
proof	drew	suit	
grew	soon	zoomed	

High-Frequency Words

eyes	moon	another
picture	single	
only	thought	

Sue needed to see
if it is true that a
cow that went "moo"
flew over the moon.

74

Sue will read to find a clue.
This book is full of cow facts.
But not a single cow flew!

Sue read about moon facts too.
It did not give proof that cows
ever came near the moon!

Sue had another clue
about what to do.
She asked an old cow
if she had ever flown over the moon.
That cow only said, "Moo."

Sue drew a picture of this cow.
She thought that wings
would suit the cow she drew.
Her hope grew that
she might soon learn if cows flew.

78

Sue waited and waited for
this cow to fly by.
But she soon grew tired
and her eyes closed tight.

Just as Sue started sleeping,
what do you think went by,
flying and leaping?
That cow zoomed
right over the moon!

Sally's New Puppy

Vowel Digraphs *oo, ue, ew, ui*

New	cool	Scoots	noon	moon
too	soon	chewing	blue	boot
shooed	juice	fruit	school	Woo
choose	drew	droopy	smooth	grooming
true	stoop	scoops	food	mood

High-Frequency Words

new	moon	blue
thought	single	eyes
picture	gave	

On Sunday, Sally got a new puppy. Cool! Sally named her puppy Scoots. Sally played with Scoots from noon until the moon shone in the sky. Bedtime came too soon!

81

When Sally woke the next day, Scoots was chewing her blue boot. "No Scoots!" Sally yelled as she shooed him away.

Sally had juice and fruit. In class, Miss Woo asked kids to draw. Sally thought for a single instant. That's all the time she needed to choose what to draw. Scoots!

Sally drew droopy eyes and a smooth nose. She drew fur that needed grooming. Her picture was true to life, too!

After school, Sally ran home. On her stoop, she heard Scoots barking in the house. Was he waiting for her?

Inside, Sally gave Scoots hugs and three scoops of food. Thanks to Scoots, Sally was in the best mood!

New Clues

Written by Laura Nguyen

Decodable Practice Reader 20C

Vowel Digraphs *oo, ue, ew, ui*

clue	blue	room	broom
new	noon	food	cool
juice	tooth	bathroom	clues

High-Frequency Words

hear	gave	blue
new	goes	

I hear it go tick. I hear it go tock.
Mom gave me a clue
to find her blue timer.
It said, "Go to the room
with the big broom."

The room with the broom
had this new clue in place.
It said, "Go to the room
where you sit at noon."

At the table, this new clue waited.
"Find that place
that keeps food cool."

That freezer is cold!
That food and juice are frozen.
I took that clue out!
It told me to find that place
where each tooth is brushed!

That clue in the bathroom
asked me to find
the room with blue rugs.
Which room has blue rugs?

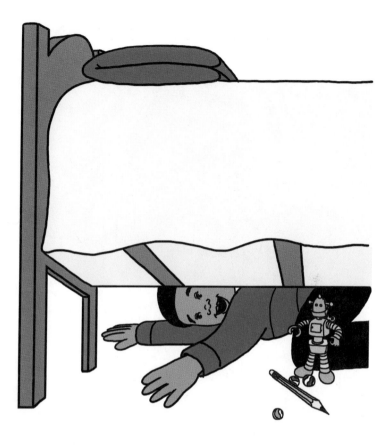

That's my room!
The timer goes
"tick, tock."
But I can't find it!

The timer went "ding!"
No new clues can be found.
Mom, show me where
the timer is now!

Restful Hobbies

Written by Dennis Michaels

Suffixes -ly, -ful, -er, -or, -ish

gardener	gladly	peaceful	restful
painter	boldly	reddish	boastful
actor	gladly	stylish	storyteller
weekly	playful	hiker(s)	bravely
teacher			

High-Frequency Words

free	enjoy	garden
anything	place	

Most people have a hobby.
A hobby is something people do
in their free time to have fun.
What hobbies can you enjoy?

Janet is a gardener.
She tends her plants gladly.
She thinks her garden is a
peaceful place.
Making plants grow is restful
for Janet.

Kelvin is a painter.
He boldly uses bright colors.
His paintings are reddish in color.
His paintings are very good,
but Kelvin is not boastful
about his skills.

Cathy is an actor.
She acts in plays.
Cathy gladly tells stories on stage
through her fine acting.
She likes wearing stylish costumes.

Ben is a storyteller too,
but he does not act on stage.
He leads a weekly story time
at a little book store.
Kids like his playful readings.

Tess is a hiker.
She has finished long trails.
She has bravely hiked up peaks.
Tess is a good teacher for
new hikers.

Anything can be a hobby.
It can be dance, reading,
arts and crafts, or sports.
Just find something that makes
you happy and have fun!

Victor's Birthday

Suffixes -ly, -ful, -er, -or, -ish

older	joyful	happily
quietly	visitor	harmful
slowly	greenish	yellowish
closer	playful	quickly

High-Frequency Words

told	teacher	you're
garden	anything	little
quickly		

It was Victor's birthday! In class, Victor told his teacher. She shook his hand. "You're getting older! Have a joyful day," she said happily.

Back home, Victor saw Mom chatting quietly with a visitor in the garden. When Mom spotted Victor, she pointed at a flower. "A harmful bug is on that flower," she said slowly. "It's greenish with yellowish wings."

Victor looked closer. He didn't see anything. And he didn't see Mom give the visitor a playful wink.

"Whoops, Victor! That little bug flew into the backyard," Mom said excitedly. "Go look quickly!"

Victor ran to the back. He found Dad standing next a greenish bike. It had yellowish wings painted on it!

Suddenly, Victor guessed that the visitor was a delivery person. The greenish and yellowish thing was really a bike. It was Victor's birthday gift!

The Helpful Gardener

Written by Jan Stroud

Suffixes -ly, -ful, -er, -or, -ish

brightly	skillful	gardener	peaceful
helpful	hardly	quickly	helper
weekly	teacher	gently	hopeful
fondly	tightly	closely	selfish
sweetly	thankful	visitor	

High-Frequency Words

quickly	teacher	told
learns	you're	little

101

"The sun shines brightly,"
Kim said to herself.
Kim's mom is a skillful gardener.
Sunny days are spent helping
Mom in her peaceful garden.

Kim is helpful.
She can hardly wait.
She quickly runs
to Mom's garden.
Kim is a good helper.

Kim and her mom work
in the garden weekly.
Kim learns from her mom.
"You're a good teacher,"
Kim told her mom.

Mom tends big plants.
Kim tends little plants.
When plants look weak,
Kim gently nurses each plant.

Mom and Kim are hopeful.
This garden is growing well.
"This may be the best garden
we have grown," Mom said,
fondly patting Kim's cheek.

Kim hugs her mom tightly.
Then she gets back to her work.
"To be a good gardener like Mom,
I will watch closely and work hard,"
Kim said. "I can't be selfish."

Kim smiles sweetly.
She is thankful for this garden.
"Every visitor will like this garden,"
she thought.

In the Woods

Written by Paula Bilika

Prefixes *un-, re-, pre-, dis-*

unlocks	unload	precooked	unties
unpacks	unhooks	unsafe	relight
unrolls	repack	dislikes	

High-Frequency Words

family	swim	hills
them	night	soft

Kenny and his family
like to go to the woods.
They camp in tents.
They swim in the lake
and hike in the hills.

Kenny unlocks the car.
He helps his mom pack.
Dad drives them to a good spot.
Then they unload tents,
full backpacks, and precooked food.

Kenny unties the ropes on the tent.
He helps his mom and dad
set up the tents.
Then Dad unpacks the food
and sets out a yummy dinner.

Kenny likes fishing at the lake.
If Dad gets a tiny fish, he unhooks
it and puts it back in the lake.
Those fish are too little to keep.

Mom puts water on the campfire
when they go hiking.
"It is unsafe to let it burn,"
Mom tells Kenny.
"We can relight it later."

114

At night, Kenny unrolls
his soft sleeping bag and slips in.
Sleep will feel good
after his full day
of hiking, fishing, and swimming.

It's time to repack the car.
Kenny dislikes litter,
so he cleans up the campsite.
He doesn't overlook anything.
Kenny can't wait to come back!

Betty's Medal

Prefixes *un-, re-, pre-, dis-*

unpacked	unable	unlike
rethought	unhappy	disliked
preteen	retrace	unfolded
rewrapped	unwrap	

High-Frequency Words

so	family
swim	soft

When Betty unpacked, she was unable to find her medal. This was so unlike her. Betty rethought her steps. That didn't help. Unhappy Betty disliked asking her family for help, but she did!

117

"I'll find it," said Sally. "I saw a show about preteen kids that find things. I'm a preteen."

"Yes," said Betty.

"Let's retrace events since you won that medal at the swim meet," said Sally.

"I just did that!" said Betty.

Then Trish spoke up. She was three. "Betty, you looked happy when they gave you that medal."

"Yes," sighed Betty.

Trish gave Betty a soft, folded napkin. Betty unfolded it and found her medal!

"At home, I found that medal and rewrapped it," explained Trish. "I wanted you to unwrap it and be happy again!"

Betty hugged Trish, "I am happy!" she said.

An Unhappy Spaceman

Written by Santi James

Prefixes un-, re-, pre-, dis-

preflight	dislikes	unlocks	reacts
unable	reclose	unmasks	unhappy
rewind	replay	reuse	

High-Frequency Words

games	those	boys
space	so	come

Jon and Jack like to
think up games.
Then they play them.
Most of the time those
boys are very silly.

120

Jon is playing a spaceman.
Jack will fly the space shuttle.
Their bedroom is a spaceship.
Jack does a preflight check
of the ship.

Jon pounds on the bedroom door.
Jack dislikes that noise.
Jack unlocks the door.
He reacts by jumping back
when he sees the spaceman.

Jack is unable to reclose his door.
What can he do so
that spaceman can't get him?
He hides behind his bed.

Then Jack acts brave.
He unmasks that unhappy spaceman.
Jack tells that spaceman to never
come back.
Jack has saved the day!

Mom and Dad got everything on film!
They rewind the film
and replay it so that
Jon and Jack can see.
Everyone laughs.

125

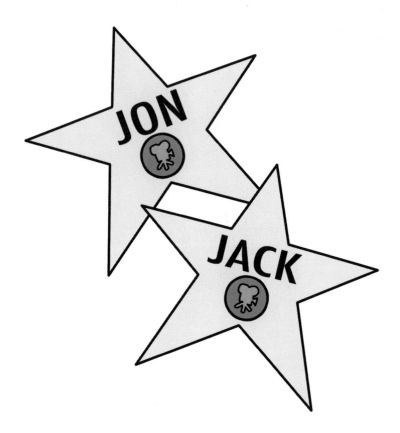

Next time Jon and Jack play,
Mom and Dad will reuse the tape
to make a funny new film.
Jon and Jack will be stars!

Writing Letters

Written by Jamie Bernsen

Consonant patterns _kn, wr, gn, mb_

write	wrote	climbed	limb
knee	wrapped	numb	knights
knots	knit	writing	thumb
signed			

High-Frequency Words

away	write	each
other	two	

127

Fred has a friend named Dan.
Dan lives far away.
Fred and Dan write letters
and tell each other a lot.

128

Dan wrote a letter to Fred.
So Fred took out paper
and wrote a letter back to Dan.
He had a lot to tell him.

"I climbed a tree and
went out on a limb.
I fell and hurt my knee.
Mom wrapped it and put
ice packs on it to make it numb."

130

"After that, Mom got me
a new game with knights,
kings, and queens," Fred wrote.
"The knights ride horses."

Fred told Dan about his camping trip.
He told about the two cats
that Mom brought home.
"I like to watch them play
on the rug," Fred wrote.

Fred told Dan that he
is learning to tie knots.
His grandmother wants
to show him how to knit too.
"It looks like a fun hobby," Fred wrote.

Fred told Dan that he had
to stop writing.
"My thumb is hurting," he wrote.
He signed his letter
and added a note: "Write soon!"

134

Camp Gnome

Consonant Patterns *kn, wr, gn, mb*

gnome	know	sign	designs
knew	write	climbed	knit
knee	wrap	wrong	Gnat
thumb	numb		

High-Frequency Words

know	other	write
man	who	

Bruce spent a week at Camp Gnome. At first, he didn't know what a gnome was. But the camp sign showed an elf. A gnome was an elf! The camp had lots of other gnome stuff. It had gnome pictures, designs, and little stone gnomes.

135

Now Bruce really knew what a gnome was!

On his third night at camp, Bruce had to write home. He told Mom that he climbed a rope. He learned how to knit a gnome scarf, too! He told that he skinned his knee. The man who was in charge of camp helped wrap it.

As he wrote, bugs flew by his head. Bruce told Mom this place had the wrong name. It should be called Camp Gnat.

After writing a bit, Bruce's thumb went numb. He signed the letter and dropped in the gnome mailbox.

Meet Tom Lamb

Written by Karen Vincent

Consonant Pattern; _kn, wr, gn, mb_

knocked	know	Lamb	wreath
sign	wrapped	wrench(es)	wrist
kneeled	knee	knob	wrong
knocking			

High-Frequency Words

truck	who
man	know

An old, white truck
pulled into our driveway.
A man knocked
on our door.

138

"I know who that is," Dad said.
"It is Tom Lamb.
He has come to fix our pipes."
Dad let the man in.

"What are you making?" Tom asked
as he pulled out his tools.
"It's a flower wreath," I said proudly.
"I made a sign that has my name too."

Tom had his arm wrapped.
My dad asked if he had hurt it.
Tom said that he had hit it
with a wrench.
His wrist was still sore.

Tom had many wrenches.
He kneeled down,
put his knee on the ground,
then lay under the sink.
Tom turned a knob.

Clink! Clank!
"Oops!" Tom said. "Wrong pipe!"
I held a wrench for Tom
while he looked closer.

When my wreath was done,
I showed Dad and Tom Lamb.
Tom was finished too.
There was no more knocking
in the water pipes.

144

Phil's Zoo Fun

Written by Alex Gardner

Consonant Patterns; ph, gh, ck, ng

Phil	back	wrong	graph
sack	Phil's	photos	phrase
pick	singing	dolphin(s)	laughs

High-Frequency Words

animals	signs
happy	cool

145

Phil likes animals.
Every summer, his mom and dad
take him back to the city zoo.
Phil can never go wrong
visiting that zoo.

First, they go in the petting zoo.
Phil likes petting the horses.
He feeds them hay.
A graph posted on the gate
shows how fast horses grow.

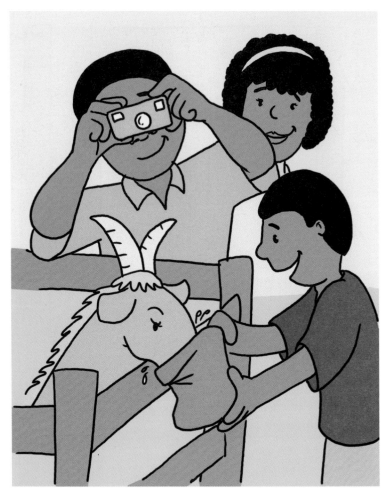

His mom gives him a sack.
It is stuffed with food
to feed the eager goats.
Those goats eat from Phil's sack.
His dad takes photos.

Phil pets a white
rabbit on the way out.
Next Phil visits wild animals.
He sees signs with the phrase
"Pick up litter!"

Hippos play in mud.
They look happy
by that cool stream.
Three foxes dart under bushes.
They are singing.

150

In the fish house,
Phil sees seastars, puffer fish,
sea horses, and sharks.
Phil likes to see
the sharks getting fed.

Before the zoo closes, Phil and his mom and dad see a dolphin show. The dolphins know how to do fun tricks. Splash! Everybody laughs.

Gramps' Photos

Consonant Patterns _ph, gh, ck, ng_

Stephen	Phil	helping	photographs
pick	checked	stacks	photos
nephews	dock	singing	laugh
rang	ringing		

High-Frequency Words

month	brother(s)
country	happy

Gramps had a big birthday this month. Mom planned a surprise party. Twins Stephen and Phil were helping.

"We will sort through old photographs of Gramps,"

explained Mom. "We will pick good photos for his party."

Stephen and Phil checked stacks of photos showing Gramps, his brothers and sisters, his kids, grandkids, and nephews. Mom found photos of him from long ago in the country. Stephen felt the best photo showed Gramps fishing on a dock. Phil picked one that showed Gramps singing on stage. The old photos made the twins laugh. They made Mom feel both happy and sad.

Suddenly, a bell rang. It sounded like Mom's phone ringing. No, it was the bell by the door. Stephen looked out the window. It was Gramps!

Phil hid the photos as Gramps came in.

Wow! That was close!

Photos From Ted

Written by Grace Peterson

Consonant Patterns ph, gh, ck, ng

rings	phone	long	photos	graphs
hang	sick	laugh	phrases	back

High-Frequency Words

brother	country	long
clean	month	

Jim has an older brother
who is in another country.
Sometimes Ted rings home
on the phone.
Mostly he writes long letters.

Ted works in hard places.
He helps people who need
clean water, food, or money.

Jim has many photos
of Ted riding in jeeps,
reading graphs, looking at maps,
and standing beside huge cliffs.

158

Ted sends photos of wild animals
for Jim to hang up in his room.
Ted sees bright snakes,
sick birds, and funny bugs.
He has even seen tigers!

When Ted sends Jim a letter, he tells stories that make Jim laugh. He teaches Jim nice phrases to say in that country.

160

Last month, it rained so much
that Ted's town flooded.
The roads were under water.
"It was hard to go places," Ted wrote.
"But now the roads are clear."

Jim read more good news
in the letter.
Ted is coming back for a visit!
Jim can't wait to be told
Ted's stories in person.

162

Fun in August

Written by Maggie Yeom

Vowel Patterns aw, au, au(gh), al

August	all	baseball	walk
always	caught	launch	taller
because	fall	falls	thaw

High-Frequency Words

stop	best
summer	walk

163

August is hot!
The sun shines all day.
I cannot stop playing
in the hot, hot sun.

164

Baseball is the best game
to play in the summer.
We walk or run from base to base.
We always know our team is good.
We win a lot and have fun.

Down at that lake
I caught a fish.
We tried to launch a boat,
but it did not float.
Maybe we'll make a new boat!

166

Mom thinks I'm always taller
at the end of a long summer.
I think it's because I run
free on sunny days
through the nice green grass.

167

When August ends,
fall will start.
First, the winds get cooler.
One leaf falls and then more come
down until no leaves are left.

168

I wait for the cool fall
and cold winter to pass.
I wait for the snow to melt
and the ground to thaw.

Then it happens.
The sun shines longer.
The grass grows again.
Summer is back!
It's time for more fun in the sun.

170

Dawn's Daughter

Vowel Patters *aw, au, au(gh), al*

Dawn	daughter	Fawn	crawling
walk	taught	lawn	fall
sidewalk	talk	ball	caught
call	Smalls	calls	paws
yawn			

High-Frequency Words

name	summer	stopped
walk	arm	mouth
best		

Dawn has a daughter. Dawn gave her daughter the name Fawn.

Fawn is just a bit past two years old. This summer, Fawn stopped crawling. Now she can walk! Dawn had taught Fawn to walk on the lawn. That way, Fawn did not fall and get hurt on the sidewalk.

Fawn can talk a bit, too! When Fawn wants a hug, she can say, "Arm!"

When Fawn is hungry, she will say, "Mouth!"

When Fawn wants to play, she will say, "Ball." Fawn has not caught the ball yet, but she tries!

Fawn can call for her pet kitty, Mister Smalls. When Fawn sees Mister Smalls do his trick, Fawn calls, "best kitty!"

Fawn likes to pet Mister Smalls on his paws. But Mister Smalls would rather just yawn and take a nap.

So would Fawn!

A Job for Paul

Written by April Rydell

Vowel Patterns *aw, au, au(gh), al*

Paul	walk	caught	awful
paw	taught	paws	because
almost	cause	always	naughty
small			

High-Frequency Words

name	tail	rains
arm	mouth	

173

Rex is my name.
I have a wet nose
and a tail that wags.
Paul is very good to me.

174

Paul must walk me each day.
He holds my leash
so that it will not get caught.
Even when it rains, we walk.

175

Paul feeds me twice each day.
When he forgets,
it's not too awful.
I paw gently at his arm
with my dish in my mouth.

Paul taught me a trick.
I stand on two paws
and hold two paws up high.
I am almost as tall as Paul!

Because I'm his dog,
I walk after Paul.
I try to walk softly,
so my paws don't cause noise.

Having me is a hard job.
I am not always so good.
But when I am naughty,
Paul stays calm
and cleans up.

When you think
it's time to get a pet,
just think of Paul and me.
It's no small job having me!

The Nicest Surprise

Written by Renee McLean

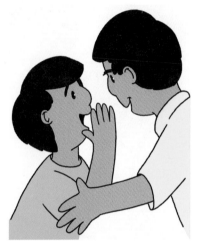

Inflected Endings -s, -ed, -ing, -er, -est

longest	planning	biggest	returns	tried
excited	helped	prettiest	tied	flowers
nicer	soaps	pointed	thinking	cleaned
cooking	making	likes	hopped	going
waved	faster	cried	rushed	peeking
called	closed	opened	nicest	coming
hugged				

High-Frequency Words

trip	surprise	returns
keep	flowers	

181

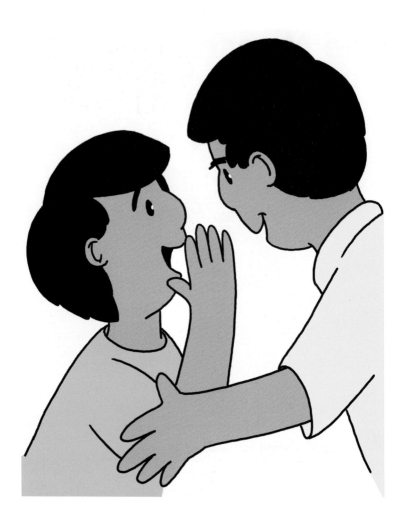

Mom was on the longest trip.
Ben and Jake are planning the
biggest surprise for when she returns.
They have tried to keep it a secret.
They are so excited!

Dad helped Ben gather the
prettiest flowers in the garden.
Ben tied the bundle.
He set his flowers on the table.

Jake put nicer soaps
in Mom's bathroom.
"Maybe she will enjoy a bubble bath,"
Jake pointed out.
"That is good thinking," Ben said.
184

Jake and Ben cleaned
while Dad was cooking.
"Dad is a good cook," Jake said.
"I hope he is making what Mom likes."
Jake went to talk to Dad.

Dad, Ben, and Jake hopped in the car.
They were going to pick up Mom!
She waved faster at them.
"It's Mom!" Jake and Ben cried.

They rushed home.
"No peeking!" Ben called.
Mom closed her eyes
as Ben and Jake led her inside.
Then she opened her eyes wide.

"This is the nicest surprise!
When I go away, I like coming
home the best!" Mom cried.
Ben and Jake hugged her tightly.

Zoo Fun

Inflected Endings

handed	printed	words	bigger
biggest	animals	exclaimed	smiled
added	papers	matches	taller
tallest	faster	fastest	shouted
slimy	slimier	slimiest	smelly
smellier	smelliest	called	looked
smiling			

High-Frequency Words

trip   but   might

Miss Bowden's class had a trip to the zoo. Miss Bowden handed each child a sheet of paper. She said, "Each paper has something different printed on it. This paper has the words *big, bigger,* and *biggest animals.*"

189

"A rhino is the biggest," exclaimed Karen.

Miss Bowden smiled and added, "In the zoo, find animals that best match words on these papers. A rhino is almost the biggest, Karen, but there might be other matches. Write them all on this paper."

The kids read their papers. "Mine has *tall, taller,* and *tallest!*" said Willie.

"*Fast, faster,* and *fastest,*" shouted Eva.

"*Slimy, slimier,* and *slimiest,*" said Ellen with surprise.

"*Smelly, smellier,* and *smelliest!*" called Walt.

The class looked at Miss Bowden with surprise. "You're going to enjoy this day," she said smiling.

The Happiest King

Written by Calvin Woods

Inflected Endings -s, -ed, -ing, -er, -est

loneliest	beasts	talking	visits	tried
talking	others	scampered	sadder	started
crying	skipping	stopped	hopping	cried
trusted	biggest	shouted	thrilled	dancing
singing	nicest	animals	danced	liked
happiest	smiles	thanks	purred	replied

High-Frequency Words

king	but
ever	afraid

Lonny was the loneliest.
He is king of this jungle,
but other beasts don't like
talking with him.
Nobody ever visits.

Lonny tried talking to others,
but most just scampered off.
Lonny got sadder and sadder.
He started crying.

Bonny Bunny came skipping by.
She saw Lonny crying.
Bonny felt afraid.
Then she stopped to think.
Why did the king cry?

Bonny started hopping toward Lonny.
"Hello!" she cried.
Lonny trusted Bonny.
He told Bonny how he felt.

"Let's throw the biggest party!"
shouted Bonny.
She was thrilled to help.
"We can plan dancing and singing.
They will see that you are the nicest."

That's what Bonny and Lonny did.
All those animals came.
They danced and sang.
Everyone liked talking with Lonny.
All of them had fun.

Lonny is the happiest king.
Now he smiles and smiles.
"Thanks so much, Bonny!"
Lonny purred.
"Anything to help," she replied.

198

Mrs. Jenkins

Written by Hannah Bayer

Abbreviations

Mrs.	St.
Rd.	Dr.
Ms.	Dec.
Mr.	Aug.
Ave.	Sept.

High-Frequency Words

important	mountain
bike	south

Mrs. Rose Jenkins works at Willis Sign Shop.
Mrs. Jenkins has an important job there.
She is the dot lady.
She paints dots on signs.

What kind of dots?
Have you seen street signs that say
"Main St." or "Mountain Rd." or
other names?
Mrs. Jenkins painted those dots!

Have you seen mailboxes that say
"Dr. Silva" or "Ms. Smith?"
The dot lady painted those dots, too.
Did she paint your mailbox?

Mrs. Jenkins paints dots on posters, too.
For example, have you seen a poster about a "Dec. 12" music concert? She may have painted that dot!

Once Mr. Ellis replaced Mrs. Jenkins
with a dot-painting machine.
That was a mistake!
It painted dots in the wrong places!

The machine did not know that "St."
meant street or that "Aug." meant
August.
Mr. Ellis sold the machine and hired
Mrs. Jenkins back.
She was happy.

So if you see a sign that reads "Bike Race! South Maple Ave. closed to traffic on Sept. 15," remember Mrs. Jenkins.
The dot lady may have painted it!

Titles

Abbreviations

Mrs.	Mr.
Dr.	Ms.
Nov.	Sep.

High-Frequency Words

north	mountain
important	almost

Anthony knew life at North Mountain School was good. But one thing made him unhappy. No one called him by a title!

In his family, his mother had a title. She was called Mrs. Delano. His dad was called Mr. Delano.

His oldest sister was an important doctor, so she was called Dr. Delano. Even his other sister who was almost thirteen was sometimes called Miss Delano. But Anthony was called Anthony or Tony or Delano.

Anthony was thinking about this in class. But Ms. Jones was explaining that month names can be shortened. For example, *Nov.* means November and *Sept.* means September.

Ms. Jones looked at Anthony daydreaming. "Mr. Anthony Delano!" exclaimed Ms. Jones. "Are you listening?"

Anthony was shocked. Ms. Jones called him by a title. But right now, it didn't make him happy!

North Hall Street

Written by Jake Swanson

Decodable
Practice
Reader
27C

Abbreviations

Sat.,	Aug.	St.
Mr.	Mrs.	Dr.
Ms.	Ave.	

High-Frequency Words

north   dog   almost

A sign said, "Yard Sale on Sat.,
Aug. 17 at 123 North Hall St."
Mr. Walter Hanks saw the sign.
He wrote down the day and
address.

At home, Mr. Hanks told Mrs.
Hanks about the yard sale.
Mr. and Mrs. Hanks planned to go.
Yard sales were important to them.

Mrs. Hanks took her dog to a vet.
Mrs. Hanks told Dr. Sara Woo
about the sale.
Dr. Woo planned to go.

Dr. Woo told Ms. Nevins.
Hall St. was close to Ms. Nevins'
house on Elm Ave.
She planned on going with her
family.

Mr. and Mrs. Hanks, Dr. Woo, and
Ms. Nevins told more pals.
Almost all of them planned to go to
the sale.
They told other people, too.

On Saturday, Mr. and Mrs. Hanks
went to the yard sale at 132 South
Hall St.
So did all a lot of other people.
But there was no yard sale!

Mr. Hanks looked at his note.
"Whoops, it's not 132, but 123
North Hall St.," he said.
And that is where all the shoppers
went!

My Future

Written by Greg Morton

Decodable
Practice
Reader
28A

Final Syllables *-tion, -ture*

future	picture(s)	mixture
action	stations	nation
locations	nature	motion

High-Frequency Words

might	paint	smile
move	take	

There are many jobs
that people have.
When I think about my future,
I try to picture what I might be.
I have many choices!

Maybe I will be an artist.
I can paint fine pictures,
using a mixture of colors.
My pictures will make people smile.

219

Maybe I will be a firefighter.
I can take action to protect my city.
Maybe I will work at stations
all over the nation!

Maybe I will be a builder.
I can make skyscrapers
and houses in many locations.
I could even make a house for myself!

221

Maybe I will be a park ranger.
I can see wild animals and enjoy
nature.
I will show people how to be safe
and keep things clean in my park.

222

Maybe I will be a dancer.
I will be in motion every day.
I will dance in shows
and teach kids
how to move nicely.

My future might hold anything!
I know that I will be happy
if I do something that I like
and that makes other people glad.

224

Future Profession

Final Syllables -tion, -ture, ion

conclusion	future	questions
pasture	sections	nature
discussion	pictures	locations
nation	action	profession

High-Frequency Words

take	paint	sections
move	nation	action
smile		

What am I going to be when I grow up? I am just seven. So I can take a lot of time to reach a conclusion. Still I like thinking about the future. I like asking myself questions about what I might do.

For example, should I be a farmer and work in a pasture? Or I might be good at house painting. I would paint top sections first and move down. Or I might be a park ranger. I like nature and hiking.

After a bit of discussion with mom and dad, I decided I might be a photographer. I snap good pictures. As an adult, I might travel to different locations in this nation and take photos of people and action that I see. Photography just might be the right profession for me.

Smile and say cheese!

Action at the Game

the Game

Written by Kelley Fulsom

My sister is taking me
to my first football game.
I can hardly wait!

228

We left the station
and walked to the school.
We found our seats
in the lower section.

"Why do those players have on
such big shirts?" I asked.
"There are pads under them," my
sister replied. "The players must use
caution so that they don't get hurt."

"This team is one of the best
in the nation," my sister mentioned.
I can tell that she is proud
of her school's team.

We saw lots of action
in this game.
It was hard to see it all
because the motion was so fast.

We saw action in the stands too.
Fans clapped and yelled for each
team. When our team captured the
ball and won, my sister jumped up
and hugged me.

233

We took a picture
with the winning players.
When I see that picture in the
future, it will remind me of the fun
we had.

234

Helpless Randy

Written by Liz Hornby

Suffixes -ness, -less, -able, -ible

lovable	useless	collectible	helpless
darkness	sadness	kindness	goodness
sweetness	weakness	fixable	brightness
colorless			

High-Frequency Words

without	life
please	back

235

This is moving day.
Sandy did not grab Randy,
her old lovable bunny doll,
when she ran out the door.

236

"Did you pack that bunny?"
Mom asked Sandy.
"He's not old and useless.
He might be a collectible."

"Randy is helpless without me!"
Sandy cried.
"Without me his life will be filled
with darkness and sadness."

238

"Please show kindness," Sandy
begged. "Let me go back for my
bunny. "Mom's goodness shone
through. She smiled because of
Sandy's sweetness.

"You know my weakness,"
Mom laughed.
"This is fixable.
We will go get Randy."

Sandy picked up Randy and
hugged him.
Brightness had come back to her face.
"We'll make you new clothes,"
she said.
"Your old ones are colorless."

Sandy got in the car
and set Randy on her lap.
Mom smiled.
Mom knew that Sandy would have
missed her good friend.

An Incredible Visit

Suffixes -ness, -less, -able, -ible

horrible	darkness	sleepless	useless
painless	restless	terrible	spotless
brightness	kindness	possible	toothless
remarkable			

High-Frequency Words

please	no	stay
small	lights	feel
back		

It was time for my trip to the dentist. I felt afraid. A dentist visit was a horrible thing. The night before, in the darkness of my bedroom, I spent a sleepless night.

That morning, I told Mom, "Please don't make me go!"

But it was useless. "No, Jane," Mom explained. "It will be painless. And I'll stay right with you!"

I was restless on the drive. "Don't be afraid," smiled Mom. "Dr. Ames is not a terrible person!"

Dr. Ames' place was small and spotless. The brightness of the lights was slightly blinding, but Dr. Ames was filled with kindness. In no time, my checkup was over. Was it possible? I didn't feel a thing! And I was afraid I would end up toothless! Now I can't wait to go back! Isn't that remarkable?

In the Darkness

Written by Joel Grand

Suffixes -ness, -less, -able, -ible

remarkable	useless	restless	darkness
dependable	brightness	helpless	readable
sleepless	kindness	edible	

High-Frequency Words

power	no	lights
small	feel	stay

There was a remarkable storm.
It knocked out our power.
We had no lights.
Many things in our house
became useless.

We felt restless in the darkness.
We went to look for things to do.
We found something that helped
us in the darkness.

Mom found a dependable flashlight.
The light was small, but its
brightness made us feel brave.
Mom and I went to explore.

248

"We are not helpless," Mom added.
"We have light, and we have
each other, so we're not lonely.
Let's find something readable."

When it was bedtime, Mom and I
went to my room.
I was sleepless.
My nightlight did not glow.
Mom stayed with me.

Mom was still in my room
when I woke.
"Why did you stay?" I asked.
"I didn't want you to be afraid,"
she said.

As I hugged Mom for her kindness,
I saw that the clock blinked on and
off. "Our power is on," Mom cried.
"No more staying in the darkness!
Let's find something edible!"

Hiking the Hard Way

Written by Lynn South

Decodable
Practice
Reader
30A

Prefixes *micro-, mid-, mis-, non-*

mismatched	midway	mislaid
misstep	microscope	midstream
nonstop	midday	misplaced

High-Frequency Words

wrong	right	were
start	stream	

Danny was so excited!
His scout troop was going hiking.
He loaded his backpack.
But things started going wrong
right away.

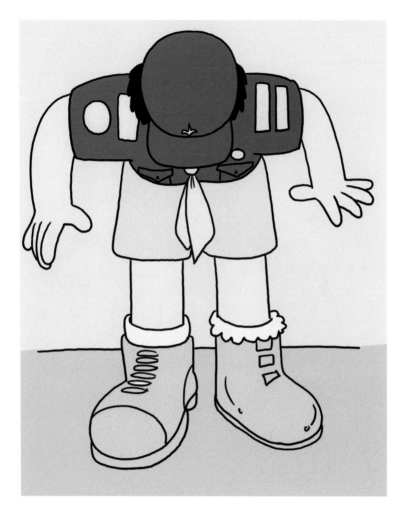

Danny put on his boots
in the darkness.
When he got on the bus,
Danny looked down.
His boots were mismatched!

Midway through the bus trip,
Danny cried, "No, no!"
He had mislaid his water bottle.
It was not in his backpack.
"I have two bottles," Kim said.

At the start of that hike,
they crossed a stream.
Danny took a misstep
and slipped midstream.
Splash! Danny broke his microscope.

Danny dried off, and they hiked
nonstop.
The hikers stopped at midday for
lunch.
Danny was happy to stop.

He looked in his backpack
for his sack lunch.
"I misplaced my lunch!"
Danny cried.
"It must still be on our bus."

Kim gave him part of her lunch.
Then they hiked back.
"I like hiking," Danny said
when he was safe on the bus.
"But it seems that hiking doesn't
like me."

Wrong!

Prefixes mis-, mid-, non-, micro

midwinter	nonstop	midnight
Midtown	midway	misread
mistake	nonsense	misprint
microfilm	misleading	misinformation

High-Frequency Words

check	latest	wrong
started	can't	right
which		

In midwinter, Ann enjoyed reading by her family's fireplace. At times, she stayed up reading nonstop until midnight! So she liked to check out books on Midtown School bookshelves.

The latest book Ann read was about the United States. Midway through the book, she saw something wrong. It said that the Pony Express was started in 1960! Did Ann misread that? No, it was mistake!

"This can't be right!" she thought. "The Pony Express started in 1860, not 1960! That's nonsense!"

Ann knew this was a misprint. Ann took the book back to Midtown School. Miss Shelly was by the microfilm. "Miss Shelly, this book is misleading." Ann said. "Can you spot which date on this page is a misprint?"

Miss Shelly spotted the mistake. "Thanks, Ann," Miss Shelly grinned. "We can't have misinformation on these shelves!"

The Midtown Market Sale

Written by Lisa Vollmer

Prefixes *micro-, mid-, mis-, non-*

midtown	midday	microwave
nonsense	misprint	misleading
midyear	midweek	midnight

High-Frequency Words

shop	can't	check
which	late	

263

Jane and her dad went
to Midtown Market to shop
at midday on Sunday.
They found a good sale
on microwaves and shirts.

264

Dad looked at a tag.
"This price can't be right.
This is nonsense.
I've never seen shirts this cheap!"

The clerk came by.
"I will check," she said.
"It might be a misprint,
which would be misleading."
She went to ask her boss.

That clerk came back smiling.
"It is right," she said.
"This midyear sale
has good prices."

Jane and Dad looked for other
good deals.
Then Dad looked at the clock.
"We have to pick up Mom,"
he said.
"We will be late if we don't go now."

"Maybe we can return midweek,"
Jane said.
"This sale ends at midnight,"
the clerk noted.
Dad looked again at that cheap shirt.

"Mom will want to see
these good deals," he noted.
"We will bring her here
while these prices are low."